BEAUTIFUL PLACES
Monticello & Jefferson County Florida

Published by Old Atlanta Publishing, LLC
oldatlantapublishing.com

Photography © Copyright 2016 by Anne Haw Holt

ISBN - 10 - 0-692-79325-9
ISBN - 13 - 978-0-692-79325-1
LCCN - 2016918026

Published by Old Atlanta Publishing LLC
oldatlantapublishing.com

Design & Layout
by Jamie Holt Sherfy

Edited by Mark Sherfy

First Edition: October, 2016

Printed in the United States of America

Dedicated to
The Wonderful People of Monticello, Florida

**Other Books By
Anne Haw Holt**

Fiction

Silver Creek
High Plains Fort
Ten in Texas
Blanco Sol
Riding Fence
Kendrick
Blood Redemption

Nonfiction

Grant Writing Step by Step
From Writer to Author

Introduction

I am a newcomer to Monticello and Jefferson County Florida. I came here alone seven years ago and fell in love with an old cottage, the beautiful historic buildings in the town and county. I made friends—wonderful friends whose ancestors settled farms and plantations in the county as early as the 1820's. Friends who love the beauty of this town and county and refuse to take it for granted.

They make my life better by saying hello when I pass them on the street. They make my life happy knowing they willingly include me in their lives although compared to their constancy in this lovely place, I am a stranger.

These friends have shown me around the town, pointed out special places throughout the county and paddled canoes for me to take photographs. Two organized an expedition into the flatwoods to find the site of the Florida volcano. Another tells me stories of the people who lived here in the nineteenth century. Even others paint a picture of the lives of Paleoindians who fished and hunted here time out of mind, leaving notes in stone to mark their passing, hidden in the rivers, mounds and sinks.

The stories and pictures in this book express the beauty of the buildings, the red hills, the always mysterious flatwoods and glorious, pristine rivers that offer a true feeling of home to every-one who loves them.

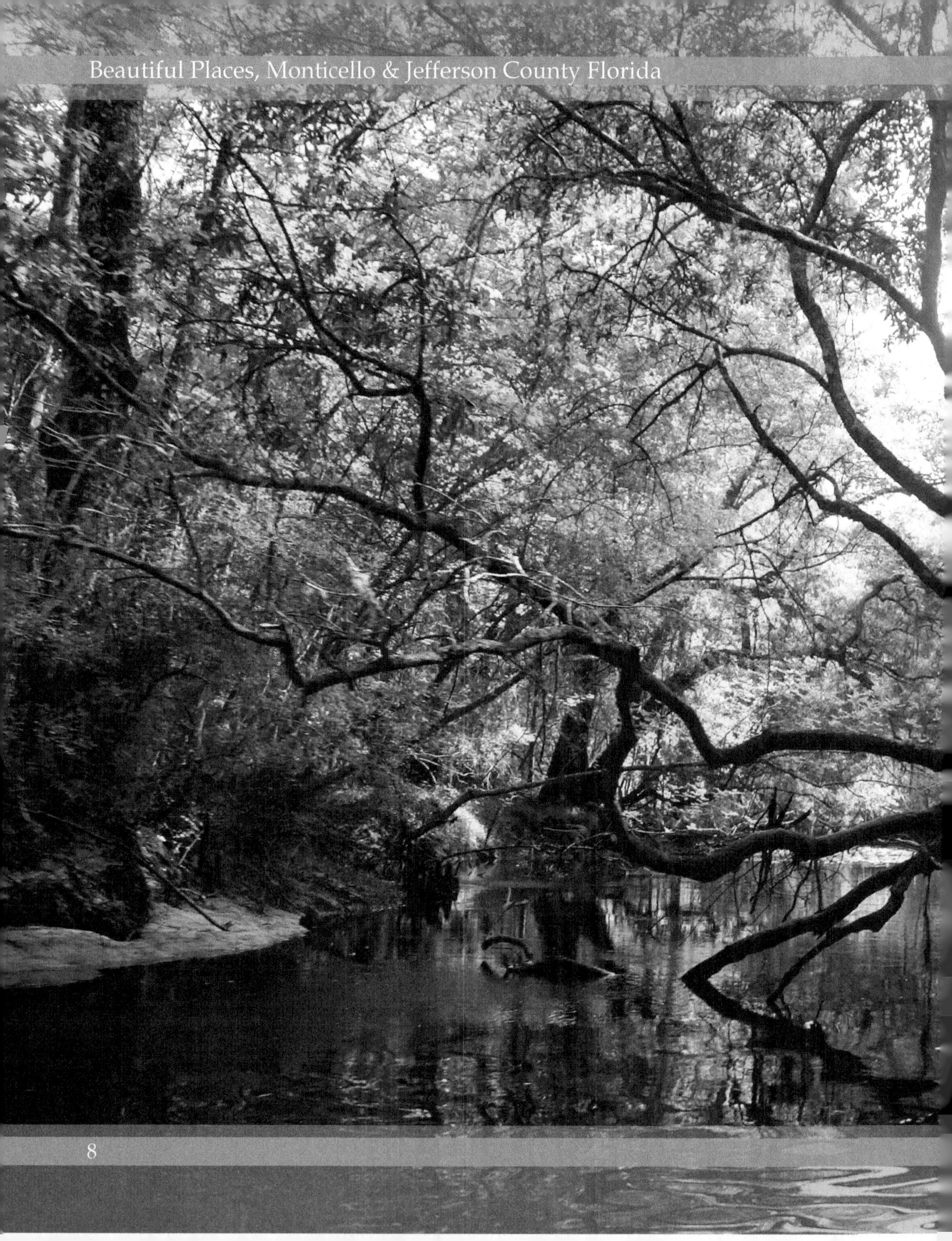

The Treasures of Jefferson County Florida

Monticello is our county seat. Eight miles away, give or take a few steps, you will find Lloyd, Wacissa, Waukeenah, Lamont, Aucilla and a couple of villages that are only a place name today, such as Ashville and Fanlew. The eight mile distance is easily explained. A horse or mule and wagon with a farmer and his family sitting atop produce or perhaps simply riding along could easily make a sixteen-mile round trip to the county seat on Saturday or Court day. Early Indian scares required an active militia, men who easily made the eight-mile trip by horseback on Thursday afternoons to drill under the Meeting Oak that still shades the south porch of our beautiful courthouse.

Jefferson County is about the 12th or 13th Florida County created in 1827, but settled earlier. A Mr. Robeson or Robertson kept a trading post here from the early 1820s. Some think a Spanish mission was located on this site. The town that grew up around the trading post was called Robeson's Corners. The town's name was changed to Monticello in 1827 and as with the county name, honored Thomas Jefferson.

Our treasures are simple, and easily overlooked until you stop and study a while. High ground, hammock to wetland, our land rolls sweetly and is covered in as many shades of green as the fields of western Ireland. This was the favored land of the Apalachees, rich farmland where they grew their sustaining crops.

The Apalachee's farming practices included burning to keep the fields clear. From the time the United States acquired the territory in 1819 these rich open fields were called "Old Fields" and avidly sought by settlers for their plantations. Men came to the area ahead of their families to select and stake out patents that included cleared and rich "old fields" that would allow them to plant a crop immediately. The first-comers didn't have to spend a year or more clearing away thick stands of pine and oak before plowing.

Jefferson County forests are still thick and dark green, full of shadows, formidably dense. The extensive flatwoods of the south part of the county are secret to all but hunters and timber men seeking stands of towering cypress—formidable and forbidding forests. Tales abound of bears, panthers and other wildlife lurking in the scrub.

There is an ancient legend of a volcano told and re-told by Native Americans and area settlers. Parties searching for the volcano tell of finding a strangely shaped hill deep in the flat woods. Huge stones are scattered about the hill. Some speculate that this hill may be the site of a peat burn or an underground gas fire. Then again, searchers may not have found the site of the volcano.

The rivers are pristine. Fed by five springs, the Wacissa's water is icy cold and delightfully clear. A short distance south of the headwaters the Wacissa is augmented by the generous flow of Blue Spring. The Wacissa is confined to the lower central part of the county and joined to the Aucilla by a canal dug by slaves. The "Slave Canal" was designed to move cotton to the Apalachee Bay for shipment to market.

The Aucilla River forms Jefferson County's eastern boundary with Taylor County. This river starts in southern Georgia, just below Thomasville and meanders the full length of the county to flow into the Apalachee Bay and the Gulf of Mexico. Not far from Lamont in the southern part of the county, it disappears underground to reappear in small, medium and large windows in the limestone locals call "Sinks."

The "Aucilla Sinks Trail" follows the underground river,

wandering from the Taylor to the Jefferson County side. Sinks range in size from simple cracks in limestone to beautiful small lakes decorated with floating islands of lilies.

The river reappears below Nuttall Rise,

running deep and wide around Ward Island, curving into Apalachee Bay and the Gulf. Along the high banks stands of cypress, mixed oak and scrub enclose and reach out into the water. As the water moves into the bay long stretches of saw grass and

clumps of palms create a disconcertingly tropical appearance.

You will pass the spot on the Taylor County side of the river where the Confederate Salt Works attracted repeated raids by the Federals. Crossing the top of Apalachee Bay the middle cut curves northwesterly and turns into the hidden Pinhook River that sweeps serenely down from the eastern flatwoods part of the Saint Marks Wildlife Refuge.

On top of our rich and treasured land and rivers--or our deep and broad history as one of the oldest towns in Florida, Jefferson County is the seat of north Florida's high southern culture. This can be experienced during a luncheon or dinner in the restored 1833 Wirick-Simmons House or the Camellia luncheon in the Budd-Carswell house. It is most obvious in the graciousness of the people, many who are descendants of the county's founding families.

Dinner on the Monticello Food Trail

I'm so thankful I was born in the South. If I hadn't been I would hire someone to teach me to speak with a Tidewater accent then I would lie. Yes, I would just plain-out lie. I'd swear I was born in Richmond Virginia or Monticello Florida. I'd have dozens of cousins and at least one eccentric uncle. My father would be handsome and my mother would be a true lady, educated somewhere like Mary Baldwin or Radford College. Southerners just know how to live.

Dinner at the restored 1833 Wirick-Simmons House in

Monticello was like taking a trip back in time—a house full of people, happy and interested, where even newcomers are treated as old friends. The lighting was a soft glow on the pale walls and high ceilings, showing off the museum quality furniture. It made the women more beautiful and the men more interesting.

The men and women of the Jefferson County Historical Association dressed the tables in white linen with crisp cloth napkins folded at each place. Polished silver utensils, a tall crystal wineglass and a stemmed silver water cup graced every plate. The candles flickered in soft breezes from the open doorways. Someone with artistic handwriting created name cards.

We talked—oh, how we talked—between each course of the delicious meal. We ate beef tenderloin done to a turn, served with potatoes, vegetables and tiny, delicious Parker House rolls. Our dessert was a piece of chocolate pie with a cherry sauce and steaming coffee.

It was obvious no one wanted the evening to end. The Wirick-Simmons House Dinner showcased our southern tradition of good food, perfectly prepared and elegantly presented to a house full of friends. Nothing could be better—it is the South at its best.

Monticello's 66th Watermelon Festival

Monticello and Jefferson County Florida will celebrate their sixty-sixth annual Watermelon Festival beginning with beauty pageants on June 4, 2016. The pageants will be followed up with events such as a great kick-off dinner (must be counted as part of the famous, deliciously satisfying Monticello Food Trail) followed up by a Bed Race on June 10. Yes, I said…Bed Race. You don't want to miss it. This traditional race is silly, funny and I found it absolutely delightful.

Have you ever thought of entering a watermelon seed spitting contest? Or have you run a race wearing watermelon Shoes? Watching your friends seriously try to win one of these events is as much fun or more than participating.

In addition to all the fun events, the town will be full of vendors selling everything from cotton candy and Kettle Korn to hot dogs and handmade handbags. You'll find pottery, jewelry, wood carving and other works of art all along Cherry, Dogwood and Pearl Streets in front of our gorgeous historic buildings.

Most small town festivals are hokey and old fashioned, but infinitely charming. This one is also surprisingly entertaining and definitely worth attending every event. Wear comfortable shoes and plan to stay late. No one does this better than Monticello…. you'll be charmed.

Watermelon Festival Schedule 2016 and **new this year**

Watermelon Contests in the Watermelon Patch

June 4th Pageants

June 10th Kick -Off Dinner, Bed Race, and new this year - Rodeo

June 11th - Rodeo

June 16th - Woman's Club Fashion Show

June 17th Arts & Crafts, Rotary BBQ, Street Dance, Kids Show - Tale of Peter Rabbit

June 18th Kiwanis 5K Run, FMB Breakfast, MADCo. Kids Show - Tale of Peter Rabbit, Platform Events, Parade, Arts & Crafts

The Flatwoods of Jefferson County Florida

The Flat Woods are a world out of time. This remote and mysterious area is almost impenetrable and unknown except by a few hunters, fishermen, and scientists. The Flat Woods are located in South-central Florida, at the edge of the Apalachee Bay and the Gulf of Mexico.

These remote tangled woods and swamps are bordered on the east by the Suwanee River and on the west by the Wakulla River. The area is split by the mysterious, disappearing Aucilla River and graced by the spring-fed Wacissa and the lost Pinhook River.

These woods and swamps boast as diverse a collection of botanical specimens as any place in the world not a rain forest. Sinkholes pierce the porous limestone underlying the jungle-like growth of oak, pine and palm, adding to the ancient mystery.

The treasures of this vast crescent, reaching almost 100,000 acres, lie deep. They are hidden from all but scientists, trained divers and special equipment. The knowledge hidden here is covered by a blanket of rotted plant life to a remarkable depth; a covering that provides anaerobic security for the remains of humans and animals waiting through centuries to tell the story of the settlement of North America.

This area has been of great interest to anthropologists, archaeologists and other scientists for many years. The evidence they have gathered through several "digs" suggests eons of settlement by humans, possibly some of the earliest settlement in North America.

The pressing question developing as evidence accumulates is whether or not the first settlers in North America came from the east or from the northwest. Could the first North American settlers have come across the ice from Europe? The answer lies waiting in the Flat Woods and its rivers, under a deep blanket of plant waste, protected by a lack of oxygen and waiting to be uncovered.

The Road To Monticello, Florida

Fred Mahan Drive links historic districts in Monticello and Tallahassee, Florida. This road started as a tribal path—became known as the Old Spanish Trail and is now Route 90, once the main east-west route across the state.

In 1935 Mahan's Nursery of Monticello, one of the largest nurseries in the Southeast, donated thousands of shrubs and trees to beautify the right-of-way along this drive. Jefferson County employed thirty-five men at 30 cents an hour to plant the shrubs, providing desperately needed jobs at a fair rate of pay for the height of the great depression.

The plantings included pyracanth, arbor vitae, crape myrtle, ligustrum and some palm trees. Recent plantings of smaller crape myrtles, from the intersection of I-10 and US 90 east of Tallahassee,

to the edge of Monticello, present a spectacular
range of brilliant colors throughout the summer months. For most
of the year the shrubs are lush and green. In winter their bare
cinnamon branches seem a work of art.

By late April and into May each year crape myrtles are
covered in deep green leaves. In May the shrubs begin to produce
large clumps of conical white flowers followed by old-fashioned
"watermelon pinks" and later the gorgeous dark reds. When the
crape myrtles are blossoming this two-lane road running east from
Tallahassee to the historic City of Monticello, Florida is a never-to-
be-forgotten treat, easily the most beautiful drive in Florida.

Local people love this highway. Once a road crew, apparently tired of mowing around bushes, started to use a huge chipping machine to "clear" the shrubbery from both sides of Rt. 90 east of Tallahassee. Late on a Friday afternoon after they cut down and chewed up a few crape myrtles, the men cut the machine off and left for the weekend.

Luckily, a reporter saw the machine devouring the crape myrtles and submitted a story to the local paper. The public outcry was unbelievable. Telephone lines seemed to catch fire from Monticello to Tallahassee to Washington, DC. Angry people called to demand help from their elected representatives to stop the destruction of the crepe myrtles.

Sometime Saturday or Sunday evening, someone cut the hydraulic lines, rendering the valuable machine useless. This action and subsequent news stories plus the frantic, angry telephone calls stopped the destruction and saved this beauty for us.

Please slow down a little and enjoy the show. You will see an occasional sturdy-looking palm tree tucked in behind the crape myrtles. You will even see a few overgrown and badly misshapen arbor vitae, but not a single pyracantha.

Monticello: Seat of Jefferson County Florida

Originating as an Indian Trading Post called Robeson's Corners, Monticello and Jefferson County were officially established in 1827, eighteen years before Florida became a state. The town and the surrounding county were settled by families from Maryland, Virginia, the Carolinas and Georgia. Prince Murat, Napoleon's nephew was one of our early settlers. James Gadsden, Richard Call and others became Florida leaders. Many of those early families' descendants still live here.

Filled with beautiful, well-kept antebellum and Victorian homes, Monticello boasts several exceptionally handsome public buildings as well as three structures designed by Atlanta Architect Joseph Neel Reid. Monticello's quiet streets are beautifully shaded by pecan and magnolia trees and great live oaks hung with Spanish moss. Yards are green and filled with azaleas, magnificent heirloom camellias and other flowering shrubs.

Located in north-central Jefferson County at the intersection of the Georgia-Florida Parkway (Rt. 19) and the Old Spanish Trail (Rt. 90) Monticello is conveniently located a short twenty-five minutes east of Tallahassee, Florida's capital and twenty-two miles south of Thomasville, Georgia. Known as Florida's "Keystone County" Jefferson is the only Florida county that reaches from the Georgia line south to the Gulf of Mexico.

The beautiful, rolling land around Monticello is green with farms, great hunting plantations and protected conservation land, bordered by the strange, ancient, occasionally disappearing Aucilla River on the east and drained in the south by the brilliant, spring-fed Wacissa. A good part of the magnificent St. Marks Wildlife Refuge at Newport, Florida on Route 98 lies in Jefferson County.

A Hometown Hero

Monticello News like most newspapers, publishes stories about heroes. These stories are often on the front page above the fold to attract attention. They recently published the story of a great, talented baseball player from Perry, Florida who helped win the World Series.

In the same issue, the News told the story of Marine "Boots" Thomas, a Monticello/Jefferson County Florida "hometown" hero who helped raise the first American flag on the far-off island of Iwo

Jima. Thomas later died fighting the enemy on that battlefield. The story explained the rededication of Thomas' remembrance plaque and the tribute to his heroism by the Fifth Division of the United States Marines.

Along with explaining the dedication activities the newspaper quoted comments made in the ceremony by Boots Thomas' friend. This is the special kind of hero who lives right here in Monticello.

Dr. Sledge has enjoyed a productive life and made a contribution to society as many will, but his long life is different. He has told Boot's Thomas' story at every opportunity for more than seventy years. His lifetime of steadfast determination to make sure his friend and his friend's story are remembered is not only exemplary but extraordinary. It is heroic.

Sledge is heroic in the quiet way many people are, without

fanfare or notice. The way a father brings home his paycheck every week for a lifetime without complaint, although he may well be completely bored with his job. The way a mother, no matter how tired she may be, makes sure her children are safely asleep before she closes her eyes. It is a heroism that is woven into his everyday life.

I have lots of lovely friends, and I'm sure you do also. We

even have some truly close friends. I am sure they will, at times, remember us fondly—(maybe fondly). Will one of them – could one of them -- remember and make sure others remember you or me and our lives for more than seventy years?

We should all hope for one friend such as Dr. Jim Sledge. He is a true hometown hero.

Jefferson County's Aucilla River

Today, in autumn, the river is dry under the Ashville Highway Bridge. In early spring I spent more than three quiet hours in the bow of a friend's canoe, wandering among the channels, wide pools and small bays created by the overflow. I snapped photograph after photograph of water birds, the pale new leaves of rampant undergrowth and gently greening cypress forest.

In the hot Florida summer, from Lamont south to our landing near the lost town of "Cash Money" we paddled a wide, strong and full-flowing river. The water sometimes tumbled and rushed over rapids, cutting into high banks.

We found fallen trees blocking our canoes, forcing a portage through the underbrush alongside the stream. Once we pushed our

lightened canoes across a partially submerged log. Wide-winged birds flew off into the forest at the sound of our paddles. The sun sparkled on water rippling over hidden stones and swirling around cypress knees.

The Aucilla disappears underground near Goose Pasture. Rushing, it dives into the depths of a limestone labyrinth for somewhere between four and five miles. The water intermittently surfaces through windows in the rock to create tiny ponds and graceful lakes, some with floating islands made of lily pads. The "Aucilla Sinks" are bordered by a well-known hiking trail.

Near Nutall Rise the water comes back to the surface where it is joined and augmented by the spring-fed Wacissa River. From there the Aucilla flows wide and deep to wander around Ward Island, curve into Apalachee Bay and race out into the Gulf of Mexico. On the far side of Apalachee Bay, hidden in the sawgrass, we found the narrow channel of the lost Pinhook River.

Jefferson County's Lost Towns

What makes a town a town? Does it take a post office to make it official? A church? A store? A graveyard? How about a name on a map?

Someone told me about a town that once existed on the Aucilla River in lower Jefferson County called "Cash Money." What a wonderful name. I decided to search some old maps for lost towns in our county. I never found the little town of "Cash Money," but to my astonishment, I found dozens of lost town names on local maps dated from antebellum times until today.

We still recognize Fanlew as a town, although the post office, church and store are gone and only a few houses mark the place. Ashville and Lyndhurst are down to one house a piece. I found town names such as Nash, Drifton, Walker's Springs and Dills. These towns were once someone's home—at one time, Lickskillet was someone's hometown.

People tell me that whatever their name, most towns in Jefferson County were around eight miles from our courthouse in Monticello. We started out just as we are now, a farming county, and this was so a farmer and his family could make it to the county seat and back home in a wagon pulled by mules in one day's light.

Our remaining towns seem to be about eight miles apart.

Lost towns are an intriguing mystery. Why did Pinhook, Beazley, Bailey Mills, Aucilla and Jarrett disappear? It's easy to understand why Monticello no longer has two hotels and several more large stores—we used to be on a main east-west route for travelers. That traffic has moved to Routes 10 and other routes. Lamont, Lloyd and Drifton were railroad towns, some boasting several saloons. They are naturally smaller now. But what happened to Cash Money, Bunker Hill, Fort Hamilton and so many others?

Monticello Bike Fest

Fun for the whole family in Monticello on April 9, 2016. Ride along Jefferson County's Heritage Roads in a 10, 30, 60 or 100 mile race. If you don't race, simply enjoy riding at your own pace amidst the elegance of our canopy roads as you wind along an historical trail that begins and ends in Monticello. We're offering an entire day of enjoyment for all.

Join the race by calling Katrina (listen, you can hear her beautiful, welcoming smile). As usual, one of our sponsors for this wonderful event is our hometown community bank; Farmers and Merchants. We are also fortunate to work with Higher Ground Bicycle Co.

This is one in a series of bike races held on the Heritage and other interesting roads and trails that wind through the natural beauty of rural Jefferson County and our five small country towns beginning in Monticello, east to Aucilla, south to Lamont, Waukeenah and Wacissa, three historic towns nestled in farms and woods, then west to the old Railroad town of Lloyd. See you there.

Paddling the Wacissa River

The Wacissa River in Jefferson County Florida is fed by freshwater springs, forming a pristine playground for people, birds and wildlife. A short drive south of the City of Monticello, the cold flowing water is bluer than the sky and unbelieveably clear. Access is from Monticello west on Route 90 to Route 59 South and Tallahassee east on Route 90 to Route 59 south. Drive straight south on 59 to the headwaters of the river.

The park at the headwaters of the Wacissa is attractive, well-equipped and beautifully kept. Managed by Jefferson County as a public park, there is provision for picnicing, swimming and launching small watercraft. Rental watercraft are available near the park including kayaks, canoes, gunnoes and skiffs. Most craft are paddled, rowed or powered by electricity so not to frighten off the wildlife.

Many visitors take the short "Paddle" from the park to Blue Spring about one mile downriver. Watercraft are assisted by the current on the way downriver but paddling offers a mild workout on the return trip. Blue Spring is something worth seeing. The flow

of the distinctive blue water from this first magnitude spring into the river is spectacular.

The quiet river is filled with wildlife. It is often possible to see four or five water birds at a time. Take your camera. Some birds will hold their ground until you get close to their feeding area. They will then give you a show as they fly just out of your reach and settle down to feeding again. It's nothing to see several Great Egrets, a Bittern and various ducks and small waterfowl.

Ambitious Kayakers or Canoeists traveling with an experienced guide follow the river past Blue Spring to take the "Slave Canal" connecting the Wacissa to the lower Aucilla River which gives access to the Gulf.

This canal is said to have been begun by Native Americans many years ago and re-opened by slave labor in the 1850s. It was expected to serve as a barge canal to move bales of cotton to the Appalachee Bay and the Gulf of Mexico where they could be loaded on ships and sent to market. The canal was hardly finished when a railroad was built that took its place.

Small Towns Have Long Memories

An exhibit of historical photographs of "Founding Families of Jefferson County" is showing in Jefferson Arts Gallery, open 10 PM to 2 PM every Wednesday and Saturday. The free Exhibit will run through February, 2016. Many of these photographs evoke interesting memories in visitors who have lived the area for years or are descendants of our founding families.

Families from Virginia, Georgia, South Carolina started coming to the town we call Monticello around 1820. They found a few families already here, the Alexanders and others. There was a trading post kept by someone named Robeson or Robertson, perhaps located at the corner of present day Pearl and Jefferson Streets. The spot where our beautiful Jefferson County courthouse now sits was known as Roberson or Robertson's Corners.

Sometimes a man would come before his family, to find a place to develop a plantation. Wisely, he would search for "old fields," those burned over areas in the rich red hills where for many years, the Apalachee kept the land cleared and raised their corn. Siting a plantation on old fields meant a planter could raise a crop the first year, not have to wait to clear land before he could plant. That first crop could make all the difference in his success.

Monticello is an extremely small town. Respect for our town's past glory runs deep. Our shady street are simply lovely. The town is surrounded by the beautiful "Red Hills" of Florida, gracefully rolling hills that still prove congenial to small-scale farmers, breeders of Thoroughbred race horses, planters and conservationists who love the lush and inviting landscape.

The town itself still has many well-preserved houses, shops and small businesses. They all look as though they sprang up of their own accord through the course of a long and virtuous history.

Monticello and Jefferson County's long history is always with us. The descendants of families who settled here in the 1820s and before live on Washington, Jefferson, Madison and other Streets in Monticello. Plantation families live in Lloyd, Lamont, Ashville, Aucilla, Waukeenah and Wacissa. Descendants of founding families work in our shops, run small farms and businesses and serve in City and County offices. Tiny towns have long memories.

These photographs of early families evoke wonderful stories of romance, historical gossip, even tales about duels fought in the "no-man's land" along the Georgia state border. I've been told that there are two families in Jefferson County who do not speak to this day because of a duel fought before the Civil War. Oh, they say there was a Jefferson County judge who sat in the cupola of the Courthouse and played the violin on summer evenings.

Southern Music Rising Festival April 9, 2016

Saturday April 9th will be the ninth celebration of Monticello's Southern Music Rising Festival. This celebration of Southern Music is presented by The Foundation for the Preservation of Historic American Music. Some say this Festival is Florida's best kept secret. The Foundation supports and offers performances in every musical genre from Funk to Country-Western, Blues, Pop, Ragtime, Jazz, Bluegrass, Classical and everything in between. Every Festival offers a variety so you will be able to find music you love.

This year the music begins at eleven in the morning, right after the Great Monticello Bike Fest is over you'll be able to see and hear performances by newcomers such as Chris Henry and the Hardcore Grass. These musicians are followed by old favorites such as Slim Fatz, Brian Smally and Sam Pacetti. Headlining the evening show will be Atlanta's Bill Sheffield, followed by Tallahassee's The New 76ers.

Capping off this amazing collection of performers will be a gala evening of dancing to the tunes of the Allie Cats in the elegant garden of Monticello's beautiful old Opera House. The garden is located just across the circle from the Jefferson County Courthouse.

So even if you come early to ride in the Bike Fest or just watch the riders, there's something to do in Monticello all day long on this special day. Bring your dancing shoes, your favorite partner and join the fun. Restaurants and stores will be open to welcome you. For more information email – southernmusicrising.com.

Southern Music Rising Singer-Songwriter Night with Grant Peeples, Sarah Mac, & Danny Goddard and others
Music at Two Beard Farm in Monticello, Florida

Southern Music Rising events are presented by The Foundation for the Preservation of Historic American Music located in Monticello, Florida. Our events are sponsored and supported by you, our supporters, local businesses and the thousands of visitors that come to our Music Festival. The Foundation is dedicated to the economic, cultural and social quality of life in this beautiful north Florida--Southern Georgia area.

This special Singer-Songwriter event is designed to bring together music lovers and people of who love this special area of Florida and South Georgia to hear seasoned and developing singer-songwriters offer their original music – music flavored by the unique southern culture of our own part of the country.

Ours is an eclectic music culture ranging through all forms of music from orchestral to banjo to piano to voice, with every possible named music represented from old- time Country to hard Blues and Funk to Progressive Jazz, with a little bit of classical thrown in here and there. Join us at Southern Music Rising – enjoy the music and the crowd. We look forward to seeing you.

A New Kind of County Fair

The Jefferson County Fair and BBQ Cook-Off is coming to Lloyd, Florida on November 7, 2015. It's a new and different fair from the County Fairs I attended in Louisa County, Virginia many years ago, but if we all go and have lots of fun I'll bet this one will grow into a bigger, more familiar event.

The BBQ contest with $2000 in prizes (sponsored by our own FMB) sounds right. There'll be judging of the many different kinds of BBQ. That should be fun for the adults. We all have a favorite sort of BBQ now, but we might learn to like a new one.

I certainly remember pie and cake contests and lots of vendors – some were a little strange—that was one of the best things. Children will enjoy bouncy houses and we all love hay rides. Teens will win the Corn Hole tournament and chase the greased pig to win prizes.

I'll miss some of the rides in the old midway. Remember the Carousel and the Whip? Who could forget the Ferris Wheel? Can we have one next year? Louisa's fair always had a Demolition Derby on Friday night—it was fun and scary, but everyone sat on hard wooden benches and loved every minute of it.

Mama entered the quilting contest and usually brought home a ribbon. Daddy took me with him to see the 4-H boys and girls showing great Hereford and Angus bulls they raised to be cuddly pets. I especially loved the tractors and other big machines. Daddy always got me a hotdog and some cotton candy and ordered me not to get sick – 'cause Mama would fuss.

I remember that "Old-Fashioned" County Fair in my poem—
see you in Lloyd on November 7.

County Fair
We walked in the evening to our old town,
out of the quiet shimmering haze.
We threaded our way there, round and round,
through the moving, seething maze.
Voices clashed and hummed and screamed.
Red and yellow flashings beamed.
Hurdy-Gurdy carousel,
sickening, pickish, sweetening smell.
Hurry the path in darkness found,
home from the fair in Mineral town.

Jefferson County's Rivers: Florida's Frontier

We drove to Mandalay at dawn, sliding an open boat into the Aucilla. Charlie Ward handled the tiller with Jack Carswell beside him. I rode amidships to take pictures. Charlie picked out his route along the curved riverbanks as he commented,. "Sharp rocks hide under the surface of this water. One of them can rip this boat to pieces."

We entered a maze of channels between curving stretches of marsh grasses dotted with palms, twisted cedars and willows. When we reached Apalachee Bay Charlie pointed out Saint

Marks Lighthouse and the almost hidden mouth of the Pinhook. He said the Pinhook is mostly limestone under the reeds and grass. Trees rooted directly into slabs of moss-covered limestone hang over the water closing out the sun.

The river narrowed and banks came closer until our boat stopped, the keel caught on a tree fallen across the water. Grabbing a nearby limb in one hand, Charlie yanked on the side of the boat and gunned the motor, sliding us across.

We finally turned to head back through the tunnel of trees. When we came out in the open the sky was dark. As soon as we ran clear of the narrow part of the river we sped up, ignoring the danger of hidden rocks. We were unsure whether to head back to the Aucilla or make for Saint Marks by open water where we would be safe.

The sky turned purple and black, and a strong wind picked up. After a few miles of wind blowing in our faces the clouds moved on to our west. The sun came back out.

As we turned north back into the Aucilla, we saw a gathering of Wood Storks resting on the limbs of a dead tree. One turned his back and spread his wings to show his eight-foot wing span.

Overhanging tree limbs cast intricate patterns on the water. We turned left at Ward Island where Charlie stopped at a floating dock. Pointing to a path up the hill he said, "Climb up there and you'll see a real family fishing cabin. Those folks hauled every stick of lumber in here on a boat."

The weathered structure looked shabby but sturdy. A covered porch protected a line of chairs backed up to the wall. I could picture a family enjoying the solitude--adults resting on the porch and children yelling as they played in the woods nearby.

Leaving the river, we followed the same route back to Monticello. Soon Charlie turned onto a narrow lane to show us the headwaters of the Wacissa River. The Wacissa is pristine — as clear as the springs that feed it. Narrow and twisted, it is land-bound and finally disappears into the earth. Its waters connect with the Aucilla through a "Slave Canal," cut by hand in antebellum times.

A large part of Jefferson County is like these rivers, still unchanged in hundreds, perhaps thousands of years. Much of the route we covered on this trip is a land and waterscape untouched and undamaged, rare and beautiful.

My Monticello

Located in the heart of north Florida, Historic Monticello is a growing and thriving community of the arts. Monticello welcomes actors, dancers, musicians, painters, novelists, sculptors, woodcarvers, weavers, poets, puppeteers, historians, photographers and other artists and artisans with enthusiastic appreciation. Many artists come here to perform or show their work and decide to become a welcome member of our exciting arts community.

Monticello artists and artisans offer music, theatre and dance in our 1890 Perkins Opera House and a Friday night Jamboree with music and dancing. Main Street Monticello hosts Singer/ Songwriting events by local and Nashville songwriters. Musicians and music lovers from all over the country attend and enjoy our growing "Southern Music Rising" festival held every spring. As many as six stages are placed around Monticello's streets for bands. The Opera House, empty lots and even some front porches are pressed into service to present dozens of performers.

Monticello is the home of The Foundation for the Preservation of American Roots Music, Inc, the creator and organizer of the "Southern Music Rising" annual music festival and other local music events.

Jefferson Arts, Inc is made up of local artists who practice many different forms including sculpture, painting, fiber art, potting, woodcarving and photography. The art center is housed in a historic school building and includes a gallery. The Jefferson Arts Gallery, Rosemary Tree, Tupelo's and other local venues offer the work of local artists for sale.

Nationally known and local historians, novelists and other writers present their works in reading and signing events and book launches. Several sell their books through local stores. Poets read original work in our library and other venues.

A "different sort" of southern town, many of Monticello's colonial families still live here. Descendants of families who established residence in the immediate area during the late Spanish period still live nearby. Many residents are artists, retired professors and business people who visited, liked what they saw and adopted Monticello as home. These people love the slightly slower, kinder pace of their town, enjoy their neighbors, the art scene and make newcomers welcome.Officially established in 1827, eighteen years before Florida became a state, Monticello was settled by families from Maryland, Virginia, the Carolinas and Georgia. Prince Murat, Napoleon's nephew was one of our early settlers. James Gadsden, Richard Call and others became Florida leaders.

The Jefferson County land around Monticello is green with farms, great hunting plantations and protected conservation land, bordered by the strange, ancient, occasionally disappearing Aucilla River on the east and drained in the south by the brilliant, spring-fed Wacissa. A good part of the beautiful St. Marks Wildlife Refuge lies in Jefferson County.

At least four Spanish Mission sites are located in southern
Jefferson County and Archaeologists have discovered Paleo-Indian
sites occupied 12,000 to 14,500 years ago in the same area. Most
of this part of the county is full of mysterious sinkholes created
by the Aucilla sliding underground and reappearing at random.
The wilderness reaches past the hidden Pinhook River to the Saint

Marks Wildlife Refuge on the west and encompasses the Ecofina on the east.

De Soto's Route across the Aucilla River to Tallahassee

Take the low road, sometimes called the "Old Mission Road" south of Madison, Florida toward the Aucilla crossing. You pass through San Pedro Old Fields, an area of fertile pasture dotted with stately live oaks draped in Spanish moss. A historical marker is beside the road near the Mission site.

Spaniards with De Soto reported marching through a "great woods" and then spending the night in piney woods. The following day they came to the village of Agile on the east bank of the Aucilla River.

The San Pedro Old Fields were probably a "great woods" when De Soto marched through in the sixteenth century. There is no true pine forest, but the area around Greenville is mixed woods with a lot of pines. It is possible the six-hundred-man Spanish army and their host of servants, captives, hogs and horses slept in those woods the night before they reached Agile.

When the Spaniards crossed the Aucilla River they described a swampy area and much more water than we find now, but there is no doubt the Aucilla River is the eastern boundary of the province of Apalachee and fits the Spanish record. Follow a dirt road south along the riverbank to the railroad. The Apalachees continuously attacked the Spaniards as they moved through a narrow track in the woods and "red hills of Apalachee" toward the present town of Aucilla, probably the site of the Apalachee town Ivitachuco.

Country Road 158 follows the railroad track, and railroad tracks often follow the oldest roads. Continue on this route to cross U.S. 19 at Drifton to Lloyd. The Spanish described a "deep ravine" in this area where the Apalachees seriously attacked them. Just east of Lloyd you cross a short bridge over a deep ravine with steep banks and a substantial stream of clear brown water. It exactly fits the Spanish description.

Route 158 continues west through Lloyd to Capitola, four miles west. Great live oaks crowd the road and the roadbed is cut deep with long use. Next is the tiny town of Chaires, still on an old road that in historic times served as the main road from Tallahassee to St. Augustine.

In Chaires you go south to Route 27 then turn left back east a short distance to take a dirt road to the right marked "St. Augustine Road." This road heads south when you leave Route 27, but soon bears around to the west. Bordered by huge old live oaks that create a dense canopy, the roadbed has gouged deep into the earth, indicating many, many years of use.

Tallahassee is about ten miles farther west. After nearly five miles of dirt the road is again paved. As you enter the outskirts of Tallahassee a marker announces you are on the "Old Spanish Road."

NOTE:

This article follows Hudson's "DeSoto's Route." There is good argument that he crossed the Aucilla far to the south of the present town of A. I will contend that his entourage was so large when you consider soldiers, followers, slaves and animals, he may well have crossed in more than two locations.

The Page-ladson Site In Jefferson County Florida

Located on the southern edge of Florida's Red Hills, the Page-Ladson archaeological dig has attracted exploration by scientists since the 1960s. In the January 2015 issue of National Geographic Magazine an article includes Page-Ladson as one of only ten sites important for studying early human settlement in the Western Hemisphere.

Recognition of the possibilities of this site was slow in coming. S. David Webb and James Dunbar were early investigators. Michael Waters of the Center for the First Americans at Texas A&M University and others have continued studying into 2014. Several remarkable finds in the 1980s and 1990s kept scholarly interest high. An artifact found in 2013 is 14,400 years old. Subsequent

discoveries verify these discoveries.

In 2012 a gathering of scientists and scholars met to discuss the meaning and possibilities of the site in the First Floridian First American Conference in Monticello, Florida. Pre-Clovis artifacts were displayed and studied increasing lay and scholarly interest in the Red Hills Region.

Inspired by the First Floridian Conference, several scientists who were speakers in the conference and Monticello/Jefferson County community leaders formed a committee to create a local institute to support scholarly study of the Aucilla Basin.

The new Aucilla Research Institute (ARI) provides logistical and research support for visiting scientists. ARI founders expect the Institute's work to gradually spark an economic resurgence in the area. With grant funding support, the institute is involved in several explorations of the Aucilla and the nearby Gulf of Mexico. ARI participated in planning the Second First Floridians First

Americans Conference held in Monticello on October 1, 2, 3, 2015. A book of scholarly papers rising from this conference is in the process of publication by the Florida Press. A third conference, First Floridians First Americans III is planned for fall of 2018. Because of the stature of the Page-Ladson site, speakers will include some of the foremost Paleolithic scholars in the world.

C. B. Moore's excavations on the Aucilla River

Clarence Bloomfield Moore of Philadelphia, initiated archaeological investigations on the Aucilla River. In the spring of 1902 and again in 1918 Moore excavated in a Weeden Island culture mound located on the east side of the river. I will refer to this mound as Lewis Mound A. In 1918 following his excavation of Mound A Moore put several "trial-holes" in mound B and other sites along the river.

Moore published the results of his 1902 and 1918 Aucilla River investigations in the Journal of the Academy of Natural Sciences of Philadelphia (the 1902 report is in volume XII, part 2, pp. 325-330; the 1918 report is in volume XVI, part 4, pp. 564~-567). The following information comes from those reports. Moore's field notes are archived in the Huntington Free Library associated with the Museum of the American Indians (now a branch of the Smithsonian Institution's National Museum of American Indians-NMAI) in the Bronx, New York. The Lewis mounds are in Notebooks 21 and 45.

When Moore first excavated in Mound A at the Lewis farm a large portion of it was covered with a log "stable" and corral probably used in cattle ranching. At the time the 6.5-foot high mound was 64 feet in diameter. In 1918 when he returned to the site the enclosure had been removed, allowing Moore to excavate the remainder of the mound

Numerous limestone rocks from the size of a human head to irregular masses perhaps 1 foot by 2 feet by 1 foot" lay atop the mound and were found within it. The mound had been constructed in two stages; an upper zone of "clayey sand, black and tenacious, probably from adjacent swamps" overlay a 1- to 2-foot-thick stratum of packed clay. Human burials were found in both strata, all in poor shape probably because of the erosive action of groundwater acids.

In the 1902 excavations three flexed burials were found in the lower Jerald T. Milanich stratum and fifteen in the upper zone. The latter included two "bunched" groups representing eight and four people, respectively. These probably were groups of bundled remains. One flexed interment was present in the upper stratum as were two single crania. Some of these burials were covered by clusters of limestone of rocks. Also found were a chert knife or point and several shell cups with perforations (presumably Busycon cups).

Moore's 1902 excavations centered on the eastern portion of the mound. There he uncovered a cache of fourteen whole or broken Weeden Island I period pottery vessels as well as sherds from other vessels. Six of the items are llustrated in the 1902 report: a dog-head effigy adorno, a Weeden Island Punctated beaker, a Weeden Island Incised turkey vulture effigy vessel, a Weeden Island Incised crested bird effigy vessel, and two Weeden Island Plain compartmentalized vessels.

The Aucilla Sinks Trail

This Trail is part of the Florida Trail – accessible from Monticello, Florida via Route 19 south and Route 27 to Lamont, Florida in Jefferson County

The Aucilla River emerges from swamps a few miles below Thomasville, Georgia and flows southwestwardly, passing over the Aucilla Rapids (referred to as "races" by locals) and then disappears underground a half mile north of Goose Pasture Road. This underground portion of the river is known as the Aucilla Sinks Trail and designated by USA Today as one of the ten best hiking trails in the United States.

For approximately eight miles the river appears and disappears in a series of small ponds or lakes called "rises" or "sinks." The river continues this pattern until the great rise at Nutall 0.5 miles north of the US 98 bridge. The Aucilla is joined by the Wacissa near Nutall Rise and flows well straight south, around Ward Island and out into Apalachee Bay and the Gulf.

On Goose Pasture Rd., look for the Florida Trail kiosk on the south side of the road, just before the cattle grate; the Aucilla Sinks Trail follows along that portion of the river that rises through limestone windows and enters the woods to the south, just west of the kiosk. There are many sinks to follow along this trail. The trail along the River portion enters the woods on the north side of the road, a bit further west of the kiosk; the "races" are about 4 miles north of this kiosk, along the River trail.

Jefferson County's Slave Canal
connecting the Wacissa and Aucilla Rivers

My friend Ed Green took me through wilderness of the famous Jefferson County Slave Canal in a small boat. I wanted to take pictures, and he knew I was worried about my camera and believed the boat would provide more stability for me than a canoe.

The canal was beautiful, breathtaking at times, but believe me, it was a kayaking or canoe trip, not a boat trip. Although Ed's boat was small and light, it was too much for the obstacles encountered along the trail.

We slid under fallen trees, pushed over big sunken logs and made portages. Someone had done some cutting of fallen trees to open the trail, but they were obviously providing for a small canoe or Kayak not even a boat as small as ours. I'd go back any time, but I would have to go in a kayak or a small canoe. I'll just buy a waterproof camera so I don't have to worry about it.

We put the boat in at Goose Pasture. The sky was brilliant blue and the clouds were mysterious snow white shapes. We had to push through heavy grass just under the surface of the water as we moved the boat along the Wacissa toward the turn to the canal.

There are signs where the trail branches off, but you have to watch carefully, it would be easy to lose your way. I was thankful to be with someone who knew the turns.

I started taking pictures immediately. Shots from the shore alone were worth visiting Goose Pasture landing. As we drifted along the river everywhere scenes we passed seemed to be waiting to be photographed. Thank goodness for a digital camera. I would have been sick under the constraints of film.

As we entered the actual Slave Canal Ed pointed out areas of Indian mounds explaining that in this area many of the mounds are very ancient, some even Paleolithic.

It was very quiet. We began to see water birds and an occasional gator. There were two or three places where it would have been easy to take a wrong turn, but we managed to stay on the trail.

Great piles of stones, many probably two feet square, line one part of the canal. These were piled along the waterway by the hands of men working in this humid, jungle-like environment in the 1850s. It is an impressive sight, worth making the trip through the canal.

We came to the Aucilla along a stretch of water bordered by banks of wildflowers then the cabins and houses of Nutall Rise came into view and we were out of the wilderness.

Monticello's Ecological Park

Located on south Water Street, at the top of the hill beyond the old school buildings, our city council purchased 26+ acres of old growth forest to give Monticello our own "urban forest." Volunteers removed truck-loads of trash from the acreage, scoured it for invasive species removing many, and helped design trails and picnic grounds. The city found grant funding for building walks and bridges to provide access to the entire park and protect its wetlands.

If you haven't visited yet, take your children or grandchildren with you, bring your Home School group. The Ecological park a great experience. You will hear or see more than 30 species of birds including turkeys, warblers, and owls. Bird watchers have certified sightings of every ordinary bird you can imagine and a few surprise visitors. Main Street and the Chamber are working to help the City get the park on the Great Florida Birding Trail. Birding groups from Tallahassee and the surrounding area are already visiting.

A Monticello Ecological Park visit is a learning experience even for many adults but it is especially so for children. You will find signs naming trees and shrubs and signs explaining why we were so careful to protect the wetlands that actually help provide the clean, sweet water we drink right here in Monticello. I was fascinated to learn that the contractor who built the walks and bridges pushed the construction ahead of his tractor, never running a wheel into the wetlands.

There is fun in the park, not just education and exercise. You could host a luncheon on the bridge—turn right as you enter the park to find it. I attended a "brown bag" lunch hosted by Katrina and the Chamber. She placed folding tables and chairs on the bridge and we ate and discussed Monticello's needs and our future for more than an hour.

The Park's picnic area is used by the Boy Scouts on a regular basis, but it is open to you and any citizen. This area is to your left as you enter the park. The cleared picnic area boasts tables with benches and other things for your enjoyment. Extra parking is provided by our friends at the American Legion Post.

Anne Haw Holt

Anne Haw Holt, writing as A. H. Holt, is a Virginian transplanted to a 1910 "Cracker" cottage in Monticello, Florida. She attended PVCC in Charlottesville, Va. and received her BA from Mary Baldwin in Staunton, VA in 1989. She holds a MA and Ph.D. in History from Florida State University in Tallahassee, Florida.

Anne is an accomplished storyteller and photographer. She writes fiction, poetry, and non-fiction on writing, history, parenting and Frontier Florida. Dr. Holt writes grants and teaches writing, grant writing, writing and leadership.

CPSIA information can be obtained
at www.ICGtesting.com
Printed in the USA
LVOW01*0444141116

512847LV00001B/1/P